Straight Talk About...
GAMBLING

Carrie Iorizzo

Crabtree Publishing Company
www.crabtreebooks.com

Straight
Talk About...

Developed and produced by: Netscribes Inc.

Author: Carrie Iorizzo

Publishing plan research and development:
Sean Charlebois, Reagan Miller
Crabtree Publishing Company

Project Controller: Sandeep Kumar G

Editorial director: Kathy Middleton

Editors: John Perritano, Molly Aloian

Proofreader: Adrianna Morganelli

Art director: Dibakar Acharjee

Designer: Shruti Aggarwal

Cover design: Margaret Amy Salter

Production coordinator and
prepress technician: Margaret Amy Salter

Print coordinators: Katherine Berti,
Margaret Amy Salter

Consultant: Susan Cooper, M.Ed.

Photographs:
Cover: Shawn Hempel/Shutterstock Inc.; Title Page:
Ferenc Gerak/Shutterstock Inc.; p.4:Pattie Steib/
Shutterstock Inc.;p.6:MarkoPoplasen/Shutterstock Inc.;
p.8:Fer Gregory/Shutterstock Inc.;p.9:Jami Garrison/
Istockphoto.com; p.11:Shots Studio/Shutterstock Inc.;
p.12:Sweet November studio/Shutterstock Inc.;
p.15:Monkey Business Images/Shutterstock Inc.;
p.17:mikeledray/Shutterstock Inc.; p.19: ejwhite/
Shutterstock Inc.; p.20:btrenkel/Istockphoto.com:
p.22:Kzenon/Shutterstock Inc.; p.24:Shawn Hempel/
Shutterstock Inc.; p.26:siart/Shutterstock Inc.; p.30:
R. Gino Santa Maria/Shutterstock Inc.;p.33:Cindy
Hughes/Shutterstock Inc.; p.34:Elena Elisseeva/
Shutterstock Inc.; p.36:bikeriderlondon/Shutterstock
Inc.; p.38:Vicente Barcelo Varona/Shutterstock Inc.;
p.39:Monkey Business Images/Shutterstock Inc.; p.40:
michaeljung/Shutterstock Inc.; p.41:Yuri Arcurs/
Shutterstock Inc.; p.43:Hans Kim/Shutterstock Inc.

Library and Archives Canada Cataloguing in Publication

Iorizzo, Carrie
  Gambling / Carrie Iorizzo.

(Straight talk about--)
Includes index.
Issued also in electronic format.
ISBN 978-0-7787-2184-0 (bound).--ISBN 978-0-7787-2191-8 (pbk.)

  1. Gambling--Juvenile literature. 2. Compulsive gambling--
Juvenile literature. I. Title. II. Series: Straight talk about--
(St. Catharines, Ont.)

HV6710.I67 2013   j363.4'2   C2013-901016-5

Library of Congress Cataloging-in-Publication Data

Iorizzo, Carrie.
  Gambling / Carrie Iorizzo.
      pages cm. -- (Straight talk about...)
  Includes index.
  Audience: Grade 4 to 6.
  ISBN 978-0-7787-2184-0 (reinforced library binding) --
ISBN 978-0-7787-2191-8 (pbk.) -- ISBN 978-1-4271-9067-3
(electronic pdf) -- ISBN 978-1-4271-9121-2 (electronic html)
  1. Gambling--Juvenile literature. I. Title.
  HV6710.I67 2013
  363.4'2--dc23
                                      2013004905

Crabtree Publishing Company

www.crabtreebooks.com   1-800-387-7650

Printed in the USA/052013/JA20130412

Published in Canada
Crabtree Publishing
616 Welland Ave.
St. Catharines, ON
L2M 5V6

Published in the United States
Crabtree Publishing
PMB 59051
350 Fifth Avenue, 59th Floor
New York, New York 10118

Published in the United Kingdom
Crabtree Publishing
Maritime House
Basin Road North, Hove
BN41 1WR

Published in Australia
Crabtree Publishing
3 Charles Street
Coburg North
VIC, 3058

CONTENTS

It's hard to keep my folks and teachers from knowing. All these missed classes. Who cares? My grades suck. Saturday's game will make up for them. I'll just get Tammy in the school office to give me Friday's test. She owes me.

I just gotta figure out what I'm going to do about Tony. I can't duck him forever. I don't think mom and dad bought the story about my black eye. I lied. I told them I got hit in the eye with a baseball. Why wouldn't they believe me? I'm a good son.

Stealing mom's diamond necklace wasn't so cool, though. Mom thinks she lost it when they went on vacation last month. I was going to sell the necklace and give the money to Tony. Instead, I put the cash on Monday night's game. I should have doubled my money. The game was a lock. Who knew the quarterback would throw his arm out in the first quarter? I'm not worried. I'll make it up on Saturday's game.

And the hundred dollars gram gave my sister for her birthday—I'll get that back, too. Saturday's the big payoff. I'm sure of it. It has to be. If I don't win I can't pay Tony. If I don't pay him back soon, well, a black eye will be the least of my problems.

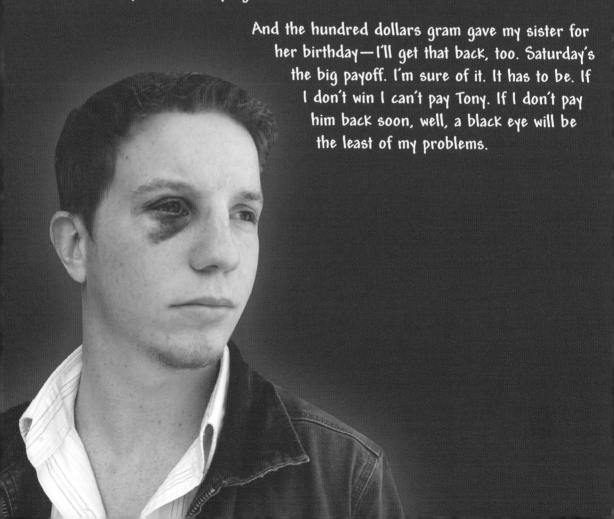

Introduction
Risky Business

Gambling, playing games of chance or betting in the hope of winning money, is a risky business. It can be addicting—sometimes from the very first bet.

In the United States, a study published in 2003 revealed that 72 percent of students in Grades 7 to 12 gambled during the previous year. Thirty-four percent said they had gambled the previous month; 12 percent said they had gambled four or more times within the month. Of those surveyed, researchers determined that 10 percent were pathological **gamblers**

The study also showed that 28 percent of students who abused alcohol and drugs also had problems with gambling. Although gambling is primarily a male activity, wagering seems to be on the rise for girls. In fact, girls now account for about 25 percent of all adolescent and teen gamblers.

"It was a game in the beginning, then I used it to kill time, then I realized it was a great escape." Michael, aged 17.

Chapter 1
Rolling the Dice

Gambling has had a long history in North America. When explorer John Cabot first landed on the shores of Eastern Canada in 1497, he found **indigenous** people playing dice and backgammon. **Archeologists** have since discovered gaming sticks that date back 6,000 years.

When the **Puritans** first arrived in America from England in the early 1600s, they immediately outlawed the possession of cards, dice, and gaming tables for at least a year. Eventually, Puritan leaders allowed church members an occasional roll of the dice, provided, of course, the game was innocent and respectable.

It's safe to say that gambling, in one form or another, has existed for a long time. Some societies frown upon it, and have made gambling, in its many forms, illegal. Although the dream of a big pay day always seems real, gambling has the potential to be an addictive game that can ruin lives, families, and futures.

Compulsive Gamblers

A **compulsive** gambler is a person who is unable to resist gambling. Compulsive gamblers fail to see the impact gambling has on their lives and the lives of others. They don't understand how the consequences

People have been playing dice for thousands of years. Archeologists have found dice in every corner of the globe. Even the early Romans enjoyed the game.

of their actions can affect their school work, their social lives, their friends, and their families.

A compulsive gambler doesn't view gambling as a way to make money. In fact, winning money is usually a secondary concern. A compulsive gambler plays for the high gambling **induces**, much like a drug addict who uses heroin or other **narcotics**.

Gambling can be a vicious cycle. The compulsive gambler will bet, and continue to bet, trying to win back the money he or she loses. They also **fantasize** about how they'll spend the money when they win big.

Games of Choice

Some gamblers will bet on just about anything, but some games and sports are more popular than others. According to McGill University's International Centre for Youth Gambling Problems and High-Risk Behaviours, the top games of chance that lure gamblers include:

- state-run lotteries
- scratch-off lottery tickets
- bingo
- pool and billiards
- card games, such as blackjack and poker
- sport lotteries and private sports betting
- casino games, including slot machines
- video gaming
- online gambling
- dice games

Bingo is a way for many churches and civic organizations to raise money. The game is also a popular way for people to gamble.

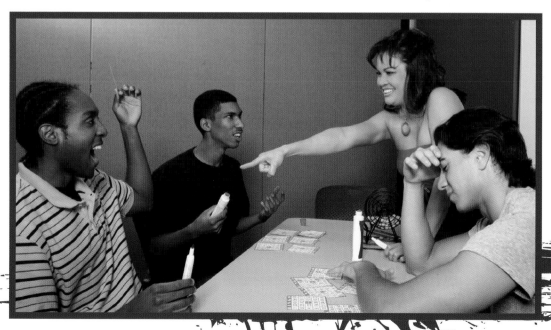

Luck or Skill?

Have you ever played bingo? How about a video or online game that required luck or skill? Nothing serious, of course, and never with money. Seems innocent, right?

Yet, gambling is gambling, whether money is involved, or whether you're playing for fun with your mom and dad. Not all gambling games are created equal, however. They fall into two categories: games of chance, such as lotteries, bingo, scratch tickets, and slot machines; and games of skill, such as poker, sports, and billiards.

Games of chance depend on luck. You don't need any special knowledge or any skill. It doesn't matter how many times you roll the dice. Each roll has the same chance of winning as the previous roll.

Problem gamblers will argue there is a **strategy** involved when playing games of chance. They play for different reasons, such as for the fun of it, the rush of winning, or to win back lost money.

Games of skill provide the gambler with some control. These games require a certain amount of knowledge. This gives you some influence over the game's outcome. In fact, the more you play, the more you increase your odds of winning. For example, the more you golf, the more likely your game will improve. As your game improves, you can bet with more confidence. The same can be said for pool, basketball, chess, and to a lesser degree, card games.

One More Hand

You might play cards for pennies or candy. It's a fun way to hang with friends, or a way to have fun with family. When the game is over and the candy is gone, you walk away.

Those addicted to gambling cannot walk away. They never want the game to end. In the mind of a gambling addict, the big win is just one card or roll of the dice away.

The gambling addict often borrows money to stay in the game. They'll sign slips of paper called IOUs to continue gambling. An IOU is a written acknowledgment of a debt between the writer and another person. A compulsive gambler will max out their credit cards, or drain their bank accounts to have enough money to play. Some will bet food money. Others resort to stealing from friends and family.

Roulette is a game of chance. It requires no special skills, only good luck.

"When I was little, Dad used to take me to the racetrack. He'd always let me pick a horse and if it won he'd give me a dollar. I remember thinking I was rich and what I was going to buy. When I was older, I started playing golf with him and his friends. I was pretty good so I started betting with the older guys and winning." Kevin, aged 27.

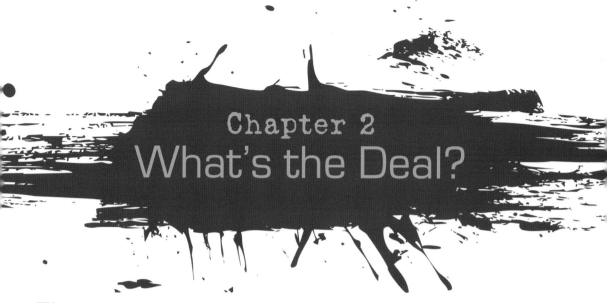

Chapter 2
What's the Deal?

The young boy's situation in this book's introduction is grave. He's having a ton of trouble. His immediate problem centers around getting more money to pay off his **bookie**, Tony, who takes bets and pays winners.

It's obvious that this boy does not understand or care about the problems he is causing his sister, his parents, and his friends. He's resorted to stealing, cheating, lying, and putting his life on the line to feed his gambling habit.

Gambling is an addictive behavior, especially for those who have problems controlling their impulses. Their behavior tends to be irresponsible and self-destructive. Individuals suffering from behavioral disorders are at greater risk for developing gambling addictions.

So, what's the draw? Don't gamblers usually lose more than they win? The answer is "yes." The cards are stacked against the gambler, whether they bet legally or illegally. The casinos, racetracks, and bookies never lose.

Placing a Bet

Why do people gamble? Some wager to win money. Others enjoy taking risks. A few gamble to escape personal problems, or to feel less lonely. Gamblers also play to cope with emotional distress, such as problems at school, abuse, grief, or family issues.

Some play to distract themselves from physical pain. Others see gambling as a way to deal with mental health issues, such as anxiety and depression. Gambling sometimes provides a temporary space and allows them to focus on something other than their problems.

According to the Gambling Institute of Ontario, Canada, there are several levels of gambling. They include:

- The casual gambler, who gambles now and then for pleasure.
- The social gambler, who is serious about wagering and gambles regularly but doesn't let it affect his or her family or life.
- The compulsive gambler, or problem gambler, who lets gambling take control of his or her life. Problem gambling can affect a person's grades, their finances, or their relationships with family and friends. It can even lead to stealing and trouble with the law.

Risk Factors

Why are certain people more at risk of becoming compulsive gamblers? Emotional problems play a huge role. Maybe you're trying to deal with a recent death or divorce in the family. You might feel depressed or anxious. Gambling helps relieve those feelings.

Maybe you have a sibling, mom, dad, or grandparent who is a gambler. Children who have been abused are more likely to gamble, as are those who have little interests outside of school. They might gamble to ease feelings of loneliness or helplessness. Gambling helps soothe their pain.

Those who have problems with alcohol or substance abuse are also at risk. The more risk factors you have, the higher your chances of becoming a problem gambler.

Having a fun evening over a game of cards with friends does not make you a compulsive gambler.

Hook, Line, and Sinker

Tanya likes to play online bingo. It's fun. She usually plays Sunday afternoons while her mom makes supper. She never plays for real money. When it's time to eat, Tanya turns off her laptop and enjoys a meal with her family.

Jeannie, on the other hand, plays bingo every day after school. She even skips her last class of the day to catch a game if the jackpot is over $1,000. Jeannie isn't doing well in school, and she's on a losing streak. She's lost so much money that she had to **hock** a pair of gold earrings that her grandmother gave her last year. Jeannie wants to keep on playing no matter what.

By the Numbers

- In New York, the two most common types of gambling are playing the lottery and playing cards.
- In Ontario, Canada, teens mostly wager on two types of card games called dare and poker.

Jeannie's Addiction

What is the difference between the behaviors of the two girls? How is Tanya's attitude toward gambling different than Jeannie's? Tanya plays occasionally and just for fun. Jeannie is addicted.

There are a number of signs that give away a gambling problem. See if you recognize any of these in Jeannie.

- Is Jeannie a person who must gamble, even though she doesn't have the cash?
- Will Jeannie sell personal items to come up with money for gambling?
- Does Jeannie miss school without a valid excuse so she can gamble?
- Will Jeannie stop hanging out with friends and withdraw from family activities?
- Does Jeannie spend hours on online gambling sites?
- Will Jeannie lie and steal to cover up her gambling habit?

Problem gamblers often sell personal possessions to finance the habit.

Easy Street?

Despite what some gamblers might think, gambling doesn't lead to Easy Street. In fact, in most cases, the opposite occurs. Look at Jeannie. She's so caught up in winning big that she sold her beloved gold earrings that her grandmother gave her. The life of a gambler is stressful and full of pain.

Jeannie is on a slippery slope and needs help. Eventually, she'll get caught by her teachers or her parents because her grades are so bad. If she continues to lose more money than she wins, Jeannie's financial woes could skyrocket. She might be forced to steal from her family or commit another crime to finance her addiction. Jeannie might one day find herself in jail.

Collateral Damage

Compulsive gambling leaves many victims in its wake. What is the **collateral** damage in Jeannie's case? Who lies awake at night and worries? Everyone who loves Jeannie—and Jeannie, herself.

Gambling is an addiction that can lead to criminal and self-abusive behavior. Friends and families of adolescent and teen gamblers often feel angry, hurt, and scared. They are concerned for their loved ones, but might feel ashamed of their gambling activities.

Stressed Out

Family members may show signs of extreme stress and burnout. Some might develop health-related problems. If there is a large debt associated with a person's gambling habit, it may trigger serious financial issues within the family. A gambler does not gamble alone. A problem gambler affects many lives.

Gambling affects everyone who loves you, especially your family, your friends, and even your teachers.

More Problems

People who are addicted to gambling are at risk of engaging in other addictive behaviors. They may feel pressured by their circle of gambling friends to drink or take drugs. Researchers say the part of the brain that responds to rewards is also influenced by gambling and alcohol abuse.

Adolescent and teen problem gamblers also suffer from depression, suicidal thoughts, problems at school, family issues, money troubles, problems with their friends, and unsafe sexual behavior. Some teens find themselves in overwhelming debt. They sell their bodies for sex to pay off the money they owe. Experts say the earlier in life a person begins gambling, the more likely they are to have gambling problems as adults.

"The casino was open all the time... I went when I didn't feel like going to class, or when I didn't want to be at home. I went when I had a lot of work to do. Every time I sit at the table, I forget about my work. I just want to be alone and be able to do my thing. I'm happy there." Michelle, aged 18.

Chapter 3
Business of Gambling

Most people view a friendly game of Saturday night cards as an acceptable social event. Many parents teach their kids how to play. Churches sponsor bingo nights. The local animal shelter sells raffle tickets to pay for the care of stray cats and dogs. Firefighters raise money to buy new equipment by raffling off turkeys.

Gambling, in one form or another, is legal in 48 U.S. states and throughout Canada. Many communities are home to casinos, horse tracks, and bingo halls. Illegal gambling is also big business. Some experts say illegal gambling is a $100-billion-a-year business.

Learning how legalized gambling and illegal gambling works is important to understanding why gambling can be such a huge problem for many people.

No Winners

Here is a fact that most casino owners and bookies will never tell you: the house always wins. The house refers to the company, or person, holding or sponsoring the gambling event. The house can be the owners of a casino, or in the case of a lottery, a state or provincial government.

You might not realize that bingo games, slot games, horse racing, scratch tickets, card games, and other forms of gambling are designed so the house never loses. Greg Fox, a computer engineering technician who works in the gaming industry, says that casino gambling machines, with their buzzers, bells, and lights, are **engineered** so you lose.

"When we work on the machines... the computers are set to pay out so much and so often," Fox says. "The house controls the odds and the payouts. The odds of winning big are not only pretty slim, they're really slim. The same goes for online games."

The machines are programmed so players eventually lose.

Legal and Illegal Gambling

Many states and provinces allow legal gambling in the forms of lotteries, scratch tickets, sports pools, and casinos. These activities are regulated by the government. Laws **prohibit** minors from participating. However, obtaining fake photo ID is easy for older teens. They give underage teens access to casinos and other gambling venues.

Illegal gambling is just the opposite. Illegal gambling is just that, illegal. It's against the law. Illegal gambling on such games as cards, dice, sporting events, and even slots, are not regulated by the government. There are few, if any, restrictions of age. In fact, many illegal games are run by teens for teens.

By the Numbers

Since the early 1800s, there have been many laws legalizing, or criminalizing, gambling in both Canada and the United States. The most recent legislation started in the 1930s in Nevada. Since then, all of Canada, 46 U.S. states, and the District of Columbia, have legalized bingo and other forms of gambling.

Betting on horse racing is legal in 42 states and Canada; betting on dog racing is legal in 19 states; casinos are legal in Canada and 48 states in one form or another; and lotteries are everywhere except in Hawaii and Utah.

Online Gambling

The Internet has changed the way people wager. Online gambling is now one of the most popular ways to bet. People can bet thousands of dollars on sporting events, poker games, and with online casinos, simply by clicking a mouse, or using an iPad or tablet.

Online casinos generate so much money that one researcher says that by 2015, online gaming **revenue** could top $150 billion. Although most online gaming sites are located in other countries, they are extremely popular in the United States, where people use credit cards to wager. It's easy for a minor to go online and bet. Although the sites ask for you to confirm that you are old enough—generally 21 years old—to bet, there is really no way to check.

Some children learn about online gambling from their parents or grandparents. It's not unusual for kids to use their parents' credit cards to play on their own.

Gambling in Private

Online gambling is often called the **crack cocaine** of gambling because it can be as addictive as the drug. Why? Online gaming allows you to gamble in private for as long as you like. The games are designed to hold your interest.

Although many sites use fake money, it's easy to bet real cash. That's because the odds of winning the free games are much higher than the odds of winning on the cash sites. The idea is to make you think the games are easy to win so you try the cash games.

Online Safeguards

Research shows that teenagers are more likely to spend their time and money on online gambling than any other type of gambling.

Web sites and governments have now developed safeguards to prohibit underage gambling. Some types of Internet gambling sites are not allowed to operate on American or Canadian soil. Still, people are resourceful. Many teens and adolescents can get around these restrictions.

"When I lose, it's really good because I am on a mission... I have something to do... try to win my money back." Jackie, aged 18.

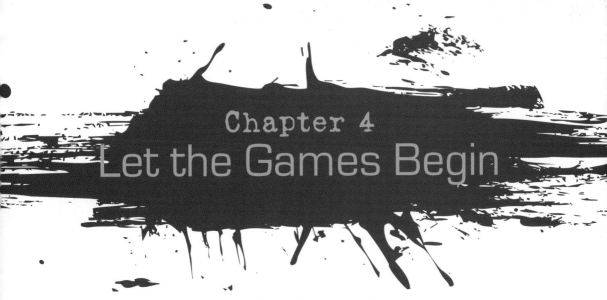

Chapter 4
Let the Games Begin

When a compulsive gambler wins, the high he or she experiences can be awesome. It can be as addictive as any drug. The excitement of winning a bet, yelling "bingo," or hitting a royal flush, is a rush. Knowing that you played it right, you called the game as you saw it, and you won, is reason enough to keep a problem gambler coming back for more.

Many gamblers consider wagering an art. They devise complicated systems and strategies to break the house. They watch carefully for the **tells** that give their opponents' poker hands away. Some look for inside information, or tips. Others study hard. People who bet on horse racing know the jockeys, trainers, and the tracks. They research a horse's past races. Everyone looks for an edge.

Myths of Gambling

Myths abound in gambling. Here are a few:

Gambling is an easy way to make money.

If you play long enough, the odds say you'll lose.

Video lottery terminals – VLTs for short – can be influenced once they start spinning.

VLTs are programmed to take in more money than they pay out.

If you play long enough you can win back what you lost.

The house wouldn't be in business very long if they lost.

"I don't gamble every day, so I don't have a gambling problem."

It's not how often you gamble, it's about how it affects your life.

"The people I gamble with appreciate me for who I am. They're my friends and I can count on them."

The only thing you can count on your gambling buddies for is to take your money when you lose. Many kids believe the people they wager with are friends, when they're nothing of the sort. Chances are these kids have a problem with gambling.

Easy Come, Easy Go

Problem gamblers dream about how they will spend their winnings if they hit the jackpot or win the lottery. These dreams and fantasies drive them to play more and bet more money.

Unfortunately, compulsive gamblers never seem to win enough to make those dreams come true. With every big win is a bigger dream. With every loss, the gambler recklessly wagers more, and the dreams become larger. Winning never keeps up with a gambler's **aspirations**.

Unknown Effects

Online gambling, also called electronic gaming, is the most addictive of all forms of gambling. Most games played online are bingo, poker, and video slots.

No one knows all the long-term effects of online gambling because today's adolescents and teens are the first **generation** to be exposed from youth to adulthood. However, research shows that teenagers are more likely to spend their time and money on online gambling than on other types of gambling.

By the Numbers

- Approximately 5.6 percent of college students have a problem with gambling. That's about 1 in 20— twice as much as the adult population.

Source: Problem Gambling Awareness & Prevention Project

"I made gambling more important than anything else. When I was gambling, I woke up every day thinking this was going to be a big day." Kirk, aged 18.

Chapter 5
I Can Stop Anytime

Almost everyone, at one time or another, has placed a bet. It might have been on the outcome of a test, a class vote, a basketball game, even getting asked out on a date. How many times have you said to a friend, "I bet you can't do this?"

Most people can make a bet, enjoy the results, and not let it impact their lives, win or lose. Others aren't able to do this.

Whether you wager fake money, or bet for fun, the rush of gambling is a high for a person addicted to wagering. They can't wait to do it again, and again, and again. In fact, a problem gambler might hit a winning streak and think, "If I'm this good, just think how much more money I can make."

Signs of a Gambling Addict

You might be addicted to gambling if you exhibit some of these signs:

- You feel a rush from the moment of your first bet, and can't wait to do it again.

- You tell lies to cover up for all the classes you miss.

- Your grades start to suffer, or you don't want to go out with your friends.

- You bet more and more money each time you gamble.

- You steal to pay for any losses, or to finance another bet.

Strategies to Cope

When you're older, someone you know may invite you to gamble. Whether that person asks you to play a hand of poker, place an online bet, or buy a handful of lottery tickets, you need to be prepared.

Be aware of the risks. Read everything you can on gambling. Do you fit the profile of a gambler? Are your risk factors high? If they are, you may want to steer clear.

If you want to play, play responsibly. Set limits and stick to them. Never bet any more money than you can afford to lose. Take only a minimum amount of money with you. Leave your debit card, credit card, and checks at home. Don't bring anything valuable with you. If you lose the money you brought, don't try to win it back.

Types of Gambling

There are four types of gamblers: social, professional, compulsive, and pathological. Social gamblers wager among friends and family. In some states, social gambling is legal.

Professional gamblers make their livings playing casino games. They concentrate on games where they believe they have a long-term mathematical advantage of winning.

Compulsive gamblers are obsessed with gambling. No matter how hard they try, they just can't stop.

Pathological gamblers have even more problems. Pathological gambling is linked to mental illness. Pathological gamblers honestly believe they can control the outcomes of the games. Their overconfidence provides a false sense of control.

A pathological gambler denies there is a problem. He or she is generous to the point of being wasteful and **excessive**. A pathological gambler believes that money can cure anything. He or she may also be a procrastinator, waiting for the last minute to do homework, chores, or study.

A problem gambler has a hard time leaving the game.

My Friend Gambles

A person can gamble responsibly and not be addicted. However, if you don't know whether a friend's gambling is getting out of hand, ask yourself these questions:

- Does my friend skip a lot of classes?

- Has my friend asked to borrow money from me or anyone else?

- Has my friend tried to sell any personal belongings?

- Does my friend have a lot of different people calling who I've never heard of?

- Does my friend hang out with the rest of our gang?

- Does my friend appear moody, nervous, anxious, or depressed?

- Is my friend always broke?

- Does my friend always have a lot of money?

- Have you caught your friend lying or stealing?

If you answer yes to some or all of these questions, your friend may need help. If that's the case, talk to your buddy, and let him or her know you are concerned.

Don't be afraid to tell a trusted adult about your fears.

It's difficult to see a friend in trouble. You might not know how to help. Express your concern, tell your friend you care, and listen if your friend needs to talk.

The Fallout

Gambling compulsively has severe consequences. Compulsive gamblers might become pathological. If that happens, they might need to get help.

The most obvious problem associated with compulsive gambling is the amount of money it takes to support the habit. Compulsive gamblers can lose many of their material possessions, including homes or cars. They can get so far into debt that they have to sell personal items for cash. Many often resort to stealing or other crimes, which can lead to jail.

Compulsive gamblers only think of one thing—the bet. As a result, their grades suffer and their personal lives disappear. They might argue with family members and become so preoccupied with gambling that they have no time for anyone or anything.

A compulsive gambler's health may suffer. Sleeping problems, anxiety attacks, depression, stress, and outbursts of anger are signs of a serious problem. The burden of a mounting debt can make the gambler feel helpless and alone. It's not uncommon to attempt or think about suicide.

"Since I placed my last bet four years ago, things have gotten better. I'm no longer spending my last dollar at the poker table. I used to live in a homeless shelter. Now, I have a credit card again. I still get the urge to gamble, but my addiction is now under control." Tim, aged 27.

Chapter 6
Getting Help

If you have access to the Internet, you can gamble. If you have friends, you can gamble. Underage gambling is a growing high-risk problem. It's not easy to predict who will have a serious gambling problem. Yet, researchers have pinpointed some factors that increase a person's chance of developing a gambling addiction.

What to Expect

Your family doctor may be one of the first people you turn to for help. To determine if you have a problem with gambling, your doctor may ask these questions:

- Have you ever tried to stop gambling but couldn't?
- Are you restless or anxious when you can't gamble?
- Do you lie to your family or friends about gambling?
- Do you think about gambling a lot?
- Does the amount of money you gamble with keep increasing?

Gambling might boost your self-esteem, but it will hurt you later on in life.

At Risk

It's not an exact science to predict who will be a problem gambler, but certain factors in your life can greatly increase your chances.

If you come from a family of gamblers you are probably a gambler, too. Males are more likely to gamble than females. Children from single-parent households or families with low incomes are also more likely to gamble.

If you've ever bet and lost more than $50 in less than 30 days, or tried gambling before Grade 8, or been pressured by your peers to gamble, then you are at risk. Teens and adolescents have a 50 percent chance of becoming gamblers, and a 1 in 4 chance of becoming problem gamblers.

Gambling can be a way to escape problems at home or to relieve loneliness, depression, or boredom. Not feeling good about yourself can also lead to gambling as a way to boost your self-esteem.

Choosing a Confidant

Once you know you have a gambling problem and want to do something about it, it's time to speak up. But to whom? Not everyone will understand. You need to talk to someone who is not going to judge you.

Choosing a person you can trust is not always easy. Your parents might be a good start. If talking to your parents is not an option, consider speaking to a favorite teacher or a school counselor. Your family doctor can provide you with names of therapists or programs that can help. You can always talk to a clergy member.

You can call a gambling hotline that specifically deals with youth gambling. These help lines allow callers to remain **anonymous** and are **confidential**.

Talking to a school counselor, a teacher, or a family physician about a gambling problem is an important step in the recovery process.

Communication

It's important to talk honestly and openly. You may be hesitant to tell a counselor the details, but he or she will help and not criticize or judge you.

If you're afraid the counselor will tell your parents, teachers, or the police, ask him or her what the ground rules are. Each state and province has their own laws regarding minors and confidentiality.

Listening and being supportive are important when helping a friend work through a gambling problem.

A Friend in Need

How do you approach a friend who you believe might have a gambling problem? What do you say? Here are some suggestions to get the conversation started.

- "You are my best friend and I really care about you. But you've been taking some really big chances lately and I'm worried."

- "If you need someone to talk to, you know you can count on me."

- "When we went out last night, I know you only meant to spend $40. I know you borrowed money from someone and lost $200. That concerns me."

- "You need to set limits when you gamble. Can you do that for me?"

Group counseling sessions are a good way to beat a gambling addiction.

Treatment and Recovery

The sooner you seek help, the greater the chance you have of kicking the habit. Serious gambling problems have the potential to last into adulthood. The types of programs for gambling addictions vary. They are broken down into two categories: outpatient and inpatient.

If you are an outpatient, you will stay at home and visit your therapist or group. Outpatient programs consist of counseling sessions or group meetings offered by organizations such as Gamblers Anonymous.

If you're being treated as an inpatient, you will live in a treatment facility for a number of weeks. A variety of in-house programs are available in the United States and Canada. Some are private. Others are run by the government.

Write it Down

Before going to see your therapist, write down the feelings you have before, during, and after you gamble. Make notes of any strong urges that started you thinking about gambling and what happened before your first gambling experience.

Write down how your life changed once you started gambling. Tell them how long you've been gambling, and what happened just before you had your first gambling experience. All this information can help your therapist understand the problem and help with your treatment.

Triggers

A trigger is an event that causes, or begins, the gambling cycle. Identifying these triggers can help stop you from gambling. Treatment will help you figure out what your triggers are and how to cope with them.

There are many ways to deal with your emotional triggers. Try waiting a few minutes to see if they pass on their own. If not, you can talk to someone until the urge passes. Sometimes thinking about the worst losing streak you ever had will discourage you. **Meditation**, walking, deep breathing, lifting weights, or spending time with friends and family are good ways to help you deal with your triggers.

You can also call your therapist, or go to a group meeting such as those held by Gamblers Anonymous.

Relapse

Sometimes the need to gamble is too great, even if you've been doing well during treatment. Any number of unexpected events can trigger a relapse. A relapse means going back to the way you were after seeming to make a recovery. A relapse is normal. The trick is to get back into recovery as quickly as possible. Don't beat yourself up. A lot of people have more than one relapse and they still manage to stop gambling.

Like any addiction, problem gambling needs a lifelong commitment. You can stop. The sooner you seek treatment, the easier the process is.

Getting your gambling under control feels wonderful. It takes work, but you can do it.

What type of gambling has the highest rate of problem gambling?

A: Of all games of chance and skill, Internet gambling has the most problem gamblers. The risk of having a gambling problem is nearly four times higher for those who gamble online.

Who is most likely to become addicted to gambling?

A: The highest risk population for gambling addiction are single male students. Males are more apt to play online poker. They'll also bet on sports. Females are partial to online bingo.

Why do guys gamble more than girls?

A: Researchers aren't sure why girls are less likely to become problem gamblers. Some have suggested that boys tend to play games that are more challenging. It may also be because guys tend to more attracted to risk-taking than girls.

Which is worse, a gambling addiction or a drug addiction?

A: Gambling can be as serious as a drug addiction. People who are addicted to gambling think that their wagering will somehow make their problems go away, the same as people who abuse drugs. Gambling addiction can also lead to lying, stealing, or other dangerous activities that could lead to jail time.

At what age do most kids start gambling?

A: Researchers say that most youth gamblers begin around the age of 10. The earlier gambling starts, the more likely you'll become a problem gambler.

Are there mental health problems associated with problem gambling?

A: Yes. A study in New York state shows that 76 percent of all gamblers suffer from depression. It also seems that gambling addicts are more likely to commit suicide than any other addictive group. Teens with gambling problems are also more likely to drink, have unsafe sex, and abuse drugs.

What is a binge gambler?

A: A person who gambles periodically and then abstains until the next round of gambling is called a binge gambler. During these episodes of gambling, the person shows all the traits of a compulsive gambler. In between gambling sessions, the person feels irritable, anxious, and frustrated. Making decisions becomes difficult. He or she will find it hard to maintain friendships and socialize with peers.

Other Resources

There is plenty of information on problem gambling for adolescents and teens. As you read through this information, you'll find some is reliable, some is not. The sources on these pages are helpful and credible. The information on the Web sites is valid in Canada and the United States. Phone numbers are good in either the United States or in Canada, but not both. If you do call a number outside of your area, the helpline will probably refer you to a number inside your region.

In Canada

Problem Gambling Institute of Ontario

http://www.problemgambling.ca/Pages/Home.aspx

Run by the Problem Gambling Institute of Ontario, this Web site provides much information about gambling treatment. There is a gambling quiz and interactive self-help tools.

Canada Gamblers Anonymous

http://www.gamblersanonymous.org/ga/

This site provides information about the 12-step recovery process and a way to link up with other gamblers in recovery.

Responsible Gambling Council

http://www.responsiblegambling.org/

This Web site run by the Canada's Responsible Gambling Council offers money-management tips, a section on warning signs, and a special page devoted to finding treatment in your province.

In the United States

Gamblers Anonymous

http://www.gamblersanonymous.org/ga/content/about-us

The Web site offers insight into gambling addiction, how the program works, and helplines for each state.

Youthbet

http://www.youthgambling.com/

This site has great information on youth gambling.

Hotlines

Ontario Problem Gambling
1-888-230-3505

KidsHelpPhone.ca
1-800-668-6868

Problem Gambling
1-888-230-3505

Youth Crisis Line
1-800-448-4663

National Council on Problem Gamblers
1-800-522-4700

Glossary

anonymous Unnamed

archeologist A scientist who studies prehistoric people and cultures

aspirations Hopes; desires

bookie One who accepts and pays off bets

collateral Of a secondary nature

crack cocaine Very potent cocaine in pellet form

compulsive Obsessive

confidential Kept private or secret

engineered Built

excessive Extreme

fantasize To indulge in the fantasies of imagination

generation A group of individuals born and living at about the same time

hock Pawn or trade

indigenous Living or occurring naturally in an area

induces Persuades

meditation An exercise used to contemplate

narcotics A drug that in moderate doses dulls the senses, relieves pain, and induces sleep

pathological A behavior or habit that is harmful and caused by an illness

prohibit To prevent something

Puritans A group of 16th century English Protestants that believed in strict religious discipline and a simple life

revenue Income

strategy Plan of attack

tells A change in behavior that may signal a good hand in poker

Index